73

Help in the Dark Season

ೞ

poems by Jacqueline Suskin

Write Bloody Publishing

writebloody.com

Also by Jacqueline Suskin

The Collected
Go Ahead & Like It
The Edge of the Continent Volume One: The Forest
The Edge of the Continent Volume Two: The City

First edition.
ISBN: 978-1949342024

Cover Design by Derrick C. Brown
Interior Layout by Winona León
Edited by Chelsea Bayouth, Derrick C. Brown, and Matt Phipps
Proofread by Keaton Maddox
Author Photo by Shelby Duncan

Type set in Bergamo from www.theleagueofmoveabletype.com

Printed in the USA

Write Bloody Publishing
Los Angeles, CA

Support Independent Presses
writebloody.com

For Meredith Clark—
safely seen and fully loved.

HELP IN THE DARK SEASON

HELP IN THE DARK SEASON

I.
My Parent Is the Universe

II.
Is Human Love the Light?

III.
Help in the Dark Season

We travelers, walking to the sun, can't see
Ahead, but looking back the very light
That blinded us shows us the way we came,
Along which blessings now appear, risen
As if from sightlessness to sight, and we,
By blessing brightly lit, keep going toward
That blessed light that yet to us is dark.

—Wendell Berry

I.
MY PARENT IS
THE UNIVERSE

Beauty growls from the fertile dark.

—Denise Levertov

HOW I FELL IN LOVE WITH THE EARTH

I don't remember being born,
but I did choose to come here.
A master in the dark,
my burning light.
I shot forth, hungry
for the ground and body.
I memorized my first moment of awe.
Standing above an overturned flagstone,
I stared at long nightcrawlers
worming in black soil. Inhaling
each color, mesmerized by the chance
that brought these pink lengths to life.
Their tenderness against
a thick crust that welcomed
them into fissures, into fine versions
of string sucked toward the core,
roaming blind, becoming and becoming.
Everything else was unlit space,
green grass moving in the void.
What perfection to break my heart.

HUT WOMAN—PAST LIFE

What a miraculous world it used to be,
when the population was small
and all I had to do was wait, a woman
in a hut, baby sucking my tit, poetry
carved into clay, and time
an unknown circular thing.

No

I was met with resistance
from the very beginning—
my mother said *no* to my spirit
as I floated above her.

She had a small awakening
with the arrival of milk,
and once I took hold
she enjoyed the ancient
purpose of a body crafting
another, unable to deny
the maniac delight
of life swimming inside her.

As a mother, she could
be more. She could shed herself
and become a passageway, a protector.

But with my first breath
her *no* returned.
No, this is not the look of it.
No, this is not my dream.
How could she hear
my crying beyond her own?

Put me down then, you tired
and hurt woman, watch
who hovers over me
in the night, three willing angels
who never grow weary.

MARRIED TO A PHANTOM

I was eighteen months old
when my father's brain went grey.
My mother saw him come
across the yard with my plastic puzzle,
he couldn't figure out how to place
the correct shapes in the holes.
What was a triangle
now that his mind was leaving?
His arm curled close to his chest
and he became a different man.
Married to a phantom, my mother stayed for me.
But did I have words to suggest her captivity?
I jumped on the bed and he pissed on the floor.
She followed the bus to make sure
he didn't get lost and taught him
how to cut a steak. Her older sister
was the golden child and she was the dark cloud.
So it made sense that fortune would force
her into motherhood, only to leave her
with the ghost of a love who never
helped around the house. He came back
to this realm with a new head.
It took her far too long to shake him—
so many hours of television, so many cries
of desire never answered. She fled
with burden but could no longer carry me,
though I was always underweight.

No Siblings

It's not that I was born
on a sinking ship.
My parents abandoned me
on deck as if I were a wolf
with an oar in her mouth.
I learned how to swim,
jumped in after them
dragging our vessel behind me.
I can't stop hoping for a crew.
I have only this cup
with a dead spider in it
and a song about
how many times my mother
sold the family pet. Rip it all
from memory and no one
will stop me because clarity
is a pearl lost somewhere
in the silky folds
of a very deep purse.
I found the horizon, the place
where the sun hits the water.
Who will I show it to?

A GLASS THREAD, AN ENDLESS SONG

It is possible for a father
to love his daughter too much.
The line between adoration
and sensuality is a thin, glass thread.

There is a bathtub in my memory.
There are rooms that only existed
when my body was small and soft.
Was I seven when I first
wanted to kill him in the kitchen
while cutting up a peach?

There is a bird singing all night long.
He goes through all of his calls, shrill
and lovely, low and robotic, a melodic
mystery to join me in my sleeplessness.
I keep thinking I hear another bird respond,
but if that were the case, why would
he still be singing?

I do not have to pick up the phone
for an answer. Sometimes the voice
inside the skeleton is the solution.
He can continue to beg and love too hard,
far enough away that I am untouchable.

BEAST LOVE

A drawing of my white room,
an overhead view, as if made
by a ghost. Sand dollar dipped in gold
and crushed behind the bulletin board.
In the side yard I stripped
the sword ferns
of all their leaves, pulling them
like reins to make piles
of green tongues.
In love with a beast on television,
I wrote an entire book of poems
dedicated to him. We spoke
through the pipes and plumbing.
What does it mean to adore the outcasts,
the mutts, the mangled, and at such
a young age, before one knows what it is
to be a sacrificial creature?
My best friend was a ferret.
All of the girls touched
each other in the basement.
Rubbing, dancing naked.
But I liked to sleep alone,
or with one of the dogs.
I'd spread a sleeping bag
on the bed so no one would see
the black hairs. Animals were
supposed to sleep in cages.
I had a dream that a monster killed
my parents and made me eat them.
He kept showing up every night
until I learned the magic of friendship.
I pretended to adore him
until I really did
and then he disappeared.

Before I Want My Father to Die

We are at the dining room table
and our chairs are on wheels.
This family is ending.
But I know that at some point
sex lived between them
because I'm here.

I push them closer together
and knock their knees. I want them
touching and then they'll find that arc
that comes alive between cells meant
for fitting, meant for making. I don't
want a brother or sister, they'd eat
too much of the love that's lacking.
I just want them, these parents, to be
two people who adore each other
enough to join in the curiosity of bodies.
They can't tell that I want them
to have sex, so they laugh and laugh
at my thrusting game. My father finally stands
to cut a peach in the kitchen with a big
butcher's knife. A week later my mother,
crying behind a closed door, will explain
that it's ending, but it's not because of me.

And then she'll take this back,
she'll blame the whole rupture
on my presence. I did ask to come down
from outer space, and from their flesh
I did rise. Unaware at first that I was
all powerful, but already trying
to move molecules, to make magic
happen in their hidden parts
and persuade them to fall back in
if for no one else but me.

The Jew & the Fisherman

I sat inside the white pick-up truck
with a blood red interior
and watched my mother kiss
the fisherman. They sat around
a fire eating the flesh of a shark.
His teeth were fake. Her thighs
were brown and his hand was big
enough to hold the meat of her
in his palm. My father was not
on the island, he was at temple
kissing someone else as well.
Who were these shadow people,
my guardians distracted by lips?
I didn't eat the shark. I slept
whenever we went to service
and didn't learn Hebrew.
When we finally drove south
for good, the fisherman at the wheel,
I couldn't measure my mother's sadness.
What was she leaving behind
but the bite of her failure
and a man who didn't love her?
My father said they chose to have me
after they couldn't get a loan
to start a business—
we needed to produce something.
My mother still calls it rape.
I'm a form of commerce,
the blame for sale
with a tag on my soft skull.
Everyone hates their baby at first.

THE BALANCE OF OLD AND NEW

How many rituals will it take
for me to release my parents?
I cut off my braid and give it to my father.
I try to craft a ceremony of repair,
but I just keep taking from my own body
and giving and giving and giving.
Nine slices of peach
for nine years of my life:
One in a cup of hot tea to drink
after steeping, one buried
in a wooden box full of soil,
one sewn with needle and thread,
one burnt in prayer, one turned
into a talisman, one between
my eyes, two pushed together
as I pushed my parents together
in their chairs, and one soaked in milk.

I'll build installations, visit psychics,
read my cards, get hypnotized, delve
deeper into Jungian dreams and mend
my mother's robe. I'll shave my head
and kneel naked while staining
my skin with beets. I'll eat an apple pie,
a family recipe, with my face covered in flour,
and I'll build home after home on my own.
My mother will cry and say *I never knew there was so much hurt.*
My father will say *why didn't you shave everything?*

Then I'll start over to notice whatever else is left.
Hair sent in envelopes. Blood on paper.
And all the while, the worst of it
comes clear when I cry.

KEEP IT CLOSE

I imagine two black indigo snakes
wrapped around my ankles
and thick ropes around my wrists.
Both are left over from childhood.
My mother killed the snakes in the yard
and I carry their magic as an act of honor.
In storms we tied the boats up
with looped knots around cleats
to keep them close and prevent
rocking damage. It's all about
keeping things close.
Memories close. People close.
Feelings even closer.
The cat has never seen a snake
or a boat. He sleeps soundly
beside my feet, but not touching me.
Not too close.
Your words are like air in my hand.
The way I love you is not casual
and it has nowhere to go.
It's a white toad on the trail,
rock towers piled up to surround
and protect it, cairns to kick over
so we can keep getting lost.
I have no song that will trick you,
I cannot cast a spell for our love
because the cards said
it will never be easy for me.
It will always be work
and you are too tired for that.

SALT WATER

My father called to tell me
that he didn't *have to love me anymore.*
I stood barefoot in the grove of banana trees,
wearing my pink nightgown, wondering
if they'd ever give fruit.
My mother was at the bar, Montego Bay.
I wasn't *number one anymore.*
I wrote my name in pencil
on my closet wall.
Swimming in the canal,
iguanas dove around me.
So many of my memories
are underwater.
I walked out to the peninsula
to stand atop a rock and sing
to the octopus, knowing it was wiser
than anyone at my house.
When they went fishing, I always asked them
to drop me off under the bridge for the day
and I'd watch the schools of pompano
and hammerhead move out to sea.
When no one else was speaking,
the warm water pulsed its answer
and if I was still enough
a heron would appear.

BAPTISM DREAM

Start by loving a God that lives
inside the shell of a black beetle.
Now get a little older
and become a Jew
who loves a God inside letters
that read backward on the page.
Older still and Christ comes
to teach some other version
that wipes us all clean
when we get dunked
in an above-ground swimming pool.
After, lick the plastic on the bottom
to remember what newness
tastes like. Circle back to the beetle
following a college mouthful of atheism
and revel in the way earth's creatures
easily shift the spirit into
an understanding of holiness.
This happens when balancing
barefoot on the branch of a live oak,
and while braiding Spanish moss.
But it also occurs while sleeping
in a city, dreaming of a river
where the water is so clear
that it will wash away
anyone's name,
and no one's hands
have to hold you under.

MOTHER MIRROR

I may or may not be pregnant.
My mother just visited.
I sent her on a healing retreat
in the Ojai Valley. She is a changed
woman now, transformed
after pushing her brow into the grass
and being hugged over and over.
She was healed, but we were not.
Even though she is better,
I'm still the one who mothers her.
I want my mother
to be a mother and I'm not yet
ready to be a mother myself.
I roll on the floor
and pet my own head, I speak
aloud, voicing all that lives
behind my mind. I shudder
at the sight of her old face
that doesn't look like mine.
How much of her is in me?
How do I learn to love it all?
I saw a vision so many years ago—
my mother seated in a white robe,
silvery hair, nearly enlightened.
She was happy, smiling,
and I was not a part of it.

I Died Behind the House

There is a woman on the hill.
She is pregnant and she is Light.
The house is just below her
and she shines her mirror on it
while cradling her womb.
She has always been there watching.
Behind the house, I'm dead.
This is where my body left me.
The three-headed dog of anger
stands logically to one side
and the owl of wisdom flanks
the house as well. The woman's mirror
catches the sun, shines brightly,
and I ignite. Now that I have
eyes again, now that I own my hands
for the first time, I can safely leave.

II.
IS HUMAN LOVE
THE LIGHT?

Attached to this world by
nothing more than hope,
I turned in a current
of dark dreams.

—Raymond Carver

HEART SONG

it blooms against the dark
which is the heart's constant
backdrop

—Louise Glück

At first, there is no answer
I can offer my heart. Its voice
sounds like a wasp in flight.

Protect yourself. It is no small feat
to reveal the stinging pain
of your past, to stay,
to say yes and mean it.

My desire for love keeps building
against the darkness and likens itself
to a lake in a cave—
the only way to get a good drink
is to follow the water deeper.

Be empty for one breath at least.
Silent, in a trance you'll see
that this wound is just a hole
where growth takes hold.

I listen to the comforting language
of a small snake draped
across my shoulders.
The cavern inside of me
howls its hollow song,
louder and louder until
I'm finally able to take over,
speaking the command to myself—
yes rose, open now.

THE WIFE WHO IS READY

Can a man resemble a tree?
Can a woman be like soil?
This is the allure for me, a lover's skin
the color of bark or the texture of silt.
The hum between our bodies
as they unite is the same as the hum
of the earth's burning core.
I resist and put my ear to the ground.
I'm already married to the world.
I'm the wife of the cradle that holds us all.
But the planet requires my expansion.
It asks me to shed my resistance,
so I try and open my arms to everyone.
You're the same as my beloved
bigleaf maple, as the whale breathing
in the blue depths, and your breath
is the edge of clouds, your teeth
are creek stones. We are moving
like the herd of deer, just groups
of cells traveling in unison.
I'm ready for us to stand
like mirrors before one another
in an endless state of wonder.

I'M A GREAT OFFERING OF EGGS

Push my shoulders into sand,
haul me up against the shoreline
and roll me in the waves.

Taste salt on my tongue, bite
my braid, teach me
what it is to be human
in the muddy grass.

Together we become
an entrance for all
that wants to live,
for all that begins
in our darkness.

BE PRESENT FOR IT

i.

Even the first time
it was something happening to me
and I was watching from above—
the shelf by his mother's bed
lined with romance novels,
her sheets, pink satin.

ii.

The visions were always set
in a dark room, walled off, small light.
A baby on a pedestal, just a baby.
Also, a grown woman, I was something
sacrificial and the men and women
made a line out the door, waiting
to spend just a few moments with me.
I was willing to be the focus of their touch.

iii.

Later, after the hotel room in San Francisco
where I realized I'd gone missing
in my mind, my body told me to wait.
It said *quit leaving me with someone else.*

iv.

It wasn't until I turned thirty-three
that I saw how ghostly it had become.
Sure, there was a period of liberation
in methodical mantras—*just like Adam & Eve*
I'd say over and over again while staring
at the ceiling fan. Now I need the eyes,
and most certainly the voice.
I need the safety of a presence
that can answer: *who are you*
to have me like this, so open?

You're Not a Human Being

Just as I'm waking up
from my river baptism dream, you
walk in the door with your hair down.
I can see pine needles stuck in the tangles
and know you've been roaming and rolling
in my favorite grove. You look wild, dark
under the eyes, dirt stains on your jeans.
Slightly out of breath, as if you've uncovered
the secret we've been waiting on, you say:
you're not a human being.

I get the violet taste in my mouth, sweet
and nostalgic. I climb out of bed, put on
my mother's old robe and start the kettle.
Still standing in the doorway
you watch my movements in order
to prove your point, hoping my knees
might bend backward
or a pair of wings will unfold.

You cannot break my stare with yours.
We end up back in bed, hands
pressed all over, mouths aligned,
more like people than ever before.

To Love a Woman

There is no kiss that I love more
than that of a woman. Yet, each woman
leaves too soon. About to create
our own way of touching, she admitted
to being too swept up in heartbreak
to make a story with my body.
Her soft mouth helped me
invent my definition of pleasure.
Her breath smelled sweet like carrots.
The idea was, we would speak
the same language and drive out
to the arroyo, never needing to return.
I don't know what will happen next.
She is a sacred text that I might
hold for years before finally
flipping a page. I could end up
an old woman in a black dress
standing at the counter
as the sun rises again with its orange
soak of light. And she could be
in the other room, asleep
with my cut braid
wrapped around her wrist.

Dark Shape

i. Arrival

This was the day before
the apartment burned down.
The day my friend was robbed.
The day her housemate had a seizure.
The day his mother broke her hip.
The cowboys called me—
in the middle of the night
they shot the neighbor's dog
with my rifle. It was coming
for the goats and they had no choice.

I needed a nap.
I climbed the stairs and lay atop
the sheets on my best friend's bed.
Her hot room, summer sweat, the big tree
dropping avocados on the roof.

After an hour I started saying: *Wake up,
I will wake up now, wake up NOW, wake up,
wake up, now I will wake up.*
As this wish came out in a whisper, a great
buildup of pressure started in my left eye.
I held my hand against the socket
and curled my knees into my chest,
my body the shape of an egg.
If only I could be new like an egg.

As the pain spread hot to my crown
like touching an electric fence, it arrived.
It hovered above me, a familiar
black image, a comforting weight
of shadow that I knew how to welcome.

ii. Meeting

My friend Krishna introduced me
to the idea of shadow people.
He named the darkness and told tales
about its power, said to never
speak of these lurkers, never talk
about the silhouettes or more
would come as if being called.
They first visited shortly after his warning.

I turned my room into a temple.
I knew something severe would happen there.
I lined the tall walls in floral fabric
and made my largest altar.
Mirrors everywhere. A lot of light.
This is where I first said yes to the shadow.

I went to bed wrapped in blankets
and my sleeping bag, hardly able to move.
I remember feeling trapped.
Close to asleep, I saw a shape begin to rise.
Slowly it came into view and hung itself above me.
Fear swelled in my chest and throat.
Then, I had an easy thought: Don't fight it.
And I didn't. I said: *you can have me*
and down it came to take me under.

It felt like the falling that happens
when a dream begins, like the pouring
of molasses, like drinking warm
milk, like a body entering my body.

I told Krishna about it the next day.
You said yes? You let it in?
I haven't heard of that.

iii. Blending

This time in the avocado tree room,
something shifted. I hardly took a breath.
On my back, I tried imagining your face.
I saw the apparition take a new form,
blending with your human features
all soft and southern, knotted hair
around sunken, amber eyes.
You were one with mystery, mixing
with my ghostly companion, bonding
with this haunt who visited me often.
I got you into focus and light
left the space above me. The specter
traced the lines of your skull
and suddenly you merged.

iv. Reality

The next day you showed up in person,
asking me to love you in the here and now.
We made plans to go live in the desert.
I didn't doubt for a moment all that was revealed
by the great amalgamation. I remember the first
time we met, years ago on Halloween.
I used my mind to summon you.
You walked into my room and said
Did you call for me?
I did.

THREE RIVERS

Last night, listening to you speak
about the red-winged blackbird,
I melted the tip of my boot
on the rim of the firepit.
This morning I still have sap
on the bottom of each bare foot
and blisters from dancing.
Redbud trees cover the green mountains
with a purple hue, a scattering of bruises.
Why don't they have blossoms
that match the color of their name?
The river speaks a rush
of cold words, snowmelt
reaching deep into my bones.
Opening the barn doors, I stoke
the sauna with fir logs,
and then I lay in the dirt.
I don't need my life
to change drastically, but I would
like a partner. Someone to build
a sacred bond with, who knows
the names of the plants I forget,
who follows me when I head
toward the largest peak.
Someday, let its giant weight
come down on us in unison.
For now, I'm happy to see
the alders out the window.
I watch the leaves flick and sway.
I don't need anyone else's eyes
in order to see the wind's skillful show.
Content as my body steams in the sun,
I'm still hoping you'll walk up the trail
to find the fire I've made for us.

HANDS DEEP IN THE DARK

When you came home, I was wearing
someone else's shoes. We searched
for my brown boots and finally gave up.
About to leave for our hike, my mother
showed up again and I leaned through
an open window to explain, very calmly,
that she was *not invited*. We walked uphill
and stopped at a big mound of composting soil,
full of flowers and mushrooms. I pushed
my hands deep into the darkness, laughing.
You pulled out the largest sunflower
and held it against your chest, saying
my name again and again.

No Romance

No one ever shows up
at my door dancing,
with poems pouring out.
A note written at the airport,
an album of perfect songs,
a brass ring with colored glass.
I want more, but not in a foolish way.
I want an in-sync, energetic wave.
Show me you were thinking of me
when I wasn't there. Allow me
to witness myself
as the never-ending source of inspiration
that fills your silly body
with something
that makes each breath better.

THE FALL

Why did we sleep on the floor that night?
I don't think you'd ever had sex
anywhere but on a mattress.
You told me about your late in life
circumcision and the scar I never noticed.
We talked of going to the beach
for the summer, horseshoe crabs, coconuts
and heron feathers. I brought up
the bird flu, which sparked the beginning
of the end of our relationship. I told you
about my vision of burying you
lovingly beneath the giant oak tree.
There was something so tender and natural
about this loss. I imagined mass graves
on your parents' land, because they had the space,
the swamps slowly rising to cover the bodies.
Maybe I can't love someone who is afraid of death?
I said: *We're a sickness on the earth, it'll find a way*
to shake us and I can't blame it. You stayed up all night
searching the internet, gauging how far the virus
had already spread, trying to ward off the inevitable.
I slept easy, as if I'd already known the greatest
parts of life, ready for the fall to come.

BED SHEET

You were the wolf
in the Japanese grocery store.
The secret shopper trailing everyone.
I wasn't a thief at that point, eating
warm chestnuts from a paper bag.
You followed us down the aisles,
not as an act of duty, but because
you *felt me*. My cousins yipped
and stared, curious when you'd make
your move. You waited until
the checkout line as they
bought their candy, and handed me
a salmon-colored piece of paper
on which you'd written your phone number
and work schedule for the month.
I can still see your profile, standing
on the rock by the lake, a slouching cherub,
perfect belly beneath your striped shirt.
We came close after a summer
of letters and mixtapes.
But we didn't know who we were yet
and I only liked to be touched
with a bed sheet between
your hand and my skin.

WHO WANTS TO FALL IN LOVE?

That person doesn't know which tree
is called the jacaranda and this one
doesn't like to lay in the grass.
That one will not get on a plane,
this one doesn't know how to cut
a squash properly, that one doesn't know
when the oleander is in bloom, this one
is unassuming, but never on time.
That one doesn't have the time at all.
This one uses her father's credit card
and that one sings the blues in a way
that is annoying. That one refuses
to drive and this one doesn't care
about the food he eats. One will have presence
but not stamina, one will be interested
and then change her mind, one will not give
a flying fuck when I point out
the beautiful, low hanging cloud.
This one doesn't care about
my homemade aesthetic, that one
didn't need to know that this bench
was crafted from old growth redwood,
this one has never used a hammer,
that one would rather not hear
about the place where I grew up
because she's never been there.
This one doesn't want a dog,
this one doesn't particularly enjoy
my scent, and this one thinks I kiss
with too much spit. This one yawns
when I tell a story that's somewhat long,
and this one doesn't want to join me
at the local bar—it's too dark
and all the songs they play are too old.

HUMMINGBIRD

Your house is not warm enough
for a hummingbird. No one knows
how many times he struck his beak
against the window before you found
his small body on the floor. He will
be dead by morning. Metallic feathers,
magic throat, he is an omen to remind you
of your short attention span, the focus
it takes to sip the sweetest things
yet never stop moving. You are too slow
for me to love and I wish it weren't so.
Don't stay and wait for me to become
the monster. Don't hang back to hear me growl.

BAMBOO

I got you to be my date
for the wedding at the last minute.
I wore her mother's dress
from 1975 and hid behind
your pickup truck to tie the straps.
You said: *this isn't like casting a spell.*
What you meant was, don't get your hopes up.
They embroidered the word yes
on a handkerchief for me,
because I'm always willing.
I read a poem for them under the old tree.
But you didn't fall in love with me.
You walked out into the bamboo
while everyone was dancing,
did tai chi in the moonlight
and took a nap. I found you
moving slowly, touching
the universe, unable to do
anything else but put your hand
on my brow. Who were you anyway?
Aware of my power, but closed
to the burning voice in your chest.
I decided to let you see what it looks like
when one forgets to put others first.
I wept beside you as you drove me home,
the ocean booming, making it easier.

CROSS COUNTRY

Counting hawks out the passenger window,
one balanced on the power line, two atop
telephone poles, three hovering
over spent corn fields, one crossing
the highway, another perched in the pines.

With each one, I say the word *home*
to ease my mind. This moment with you
should be celebratory but instead feels
like too much rain, a long winter.

You were meant to soothe me
like a piano. Instead, every time
I get out to stretch, I think about
running west. Everything is frozen.
Even the barn owl, struck on the shoulder.
You film me pulling out its holy feathers.
The whole action is sacrilege
and I'm already punished because
I look up and can hardly see you.

My pattern unfurling, edges
raw as linen. I won't know it for years,
until we swim together in a dirty pool
in New Orleans, laughing.

You extended your hand in the dark season,
an unspoiled lily slapped against the wall.
I still have the feathers. I wipe
the dust from them every month.

ALONE

I chop an onion
(so close to union)
to sauté in a pan on my stove.
There's nothing else cooking yet.
This is just the beginning. Our first meal.
I ask him, could you stir that for me?
Stir what, the onion?
Yes. There's nothing else to stir.
Why does this question upset me so deeply?
Because it makes me feel lonely,
like I'm still all alone.
Because it rings the bell
of my deepest wound and starts
replaying that old sentence that lives inside—
if you show anyone, in any way, that you are dumb, you will be left.

DIRT EATER

I walked through the canyons
with the wedding party.
I watched a man make fire.
I stood before two rock formations and bowed.
After the ceremony, everyone ate
mushrooms and I saw visions
of us all as cancer.
You picked me up the next day,
driving the airport shuttle.
You'd never rescued anyone before.
How did I fall in love with you then?
Sometimes it's as simple as distraction,
the songs on the radio, tattoos, and weird sandals.
When you came to visit, I was far too hungry.
You sat on the edge of my bed and ate dirt
from a Tupperware container but wouldn't
have sex with me. It was a dry summer,
everything was burning.

MISSING

You'll only ever be
halfway understood.
Your new girlfriend can't know
what it means to be from our island.
She's never docked a boat
or stubbed her toe on a metal cleat.
I had two dreams about your dad in one week.
First, he warned me about a sewage spill
in the Everglades, but I was too late.
I watched the dirty water
swallow an entire ecosystem.
In the second dream
he drove us around the country, made us
sit in the backseat together
so we'd fall in love again
and after a few hours
it worked.
Our song came on the radio
and you laughed at its cowboy lyrics,
its phrasing that trots
like a housecat does
when dinner is served.
We pulled over on the edge
of a mountain road, and your dad
was so impressed that I could pee standing up.
In waking life, I can't do that,
and we'll never be the yin-yang,
we'll never touch
a conch shell in unison.
You won't miss me
and I won't miss you.

TO LOVE A MAN & HIS FAMILY

We walked the trail between radio towers
and I heard a frequency say
you'll be with him when he dies.
I thought this meant I had to stay.

We agreed his cabin was a place
for therapeutic brutality.
Were we being punished?
Should I have put my mouth on the woodstove?
We tried to solve it all by having sex.
This is when I discovered the ancient eye
of an alien in my mind, staring
with a straightforward command:
you're done here.

A year later, I study the constellation
chart of Scorpio. Who gave me
this starry map pinned above my altar?
It's a gift from his ex.
I pretend she is standing here before me.
She is naked and crying.
I cover her with sage smoke.
Then her small son appears.
I hold him in my lap and fill
his body-brain with love.
I apologize for disappearing
and absolve myself
in burning leaves, candles lit,
a circle around them for protection.

NOT HAUNTED

I thought you were in love
with your mother. I remember
a dragonfly on your brother's lip.
I remember biting your chest
so hard I saw stars.
Instead of growing up and opening
a school together, you decided
to become a doctor and I left you
for a maniac who hopped trains.
There was never anyone
better than you, eyes like crystal,
radical breast bone, a question
always living on your tongue.
I thought you'd haunt me for years.
You became a Buddhist and I rode
my bicycle through the streets
of New Orleans to meet you
and your new girlfriend.
On the way I ripped my pants,
the cuff caught in the chain.
The three of us swam naked in the pool
and I finally stopped wanting you.
This girl was much softer than I'd ever be.
Finally far enough away from your home,
I thought about your mother's strong
arms, her critical gaze, and realized
that I was the one most like her,
and you were not in love.

Chicago When the Floor Broke

I was the performance artist in an experimental noise band
called *The Ear is the Brain*. My friend Krishna played the role
of the butcher and I was the seamstress—he cut and I mended,
he thrashed through guitar sounds while I danced and twisted
my body in symbolic healing gestures. We toured the Midwest.
I scraped my knees on concrete floors, slept in strangers' rooms,
and in Chicago I met the boy with the zebra bandana.
That was the night we performed for five hundred people
because the floor broke at another venue. I was standing
on a pile of bricks, sweaty, in my torn red show tights.
He hadn't seen me dance. He rode me home on the handle bars
of his bicycle, also zebra striped. A sculptor, he lived in a warehouse, fed me
fried chicken, let me shower, and his cats were named Franny and Zooey.
He fucked me standing up in his room and told me he'd done this before
with a dancer he used to date. I wasn't upset. The wall was decorated
with a wedding dress that was full of lights and hundreds of deer antlers.
In the morning, we each drove one of his zebra painted scooters
through the streets, ate Italian sandwiches, and said goodbye.
I held on in a young way, wanting more,
but months later I called him from a museum in Seattle to say
your work should be on the walls of this place and then I let him go.
I like the way a memory can be a cup worth carrying, full
of a person I don't need,
as weightless as a photo.

Spirits in the Void

I can't remember who
was resurrected first,
or which story built the foundation
for all the other stories.
In my hand is the snake skin
and a mirror. This is a circular track.
I'm standing in a familiar place.
Golden hay. Sunflowers. Corn.
You're in a long, dark cloak
and I can't tell if you're the Fool or the King of Cups.
How do you keep finding me here?
We live on the same planet.
We're in an open field, so nothing obstructs my view.
I continue to believe that it's different,
each time I trust in the miraculous, a match
of spirits in the void. Am I uttering
the same spell over and over again?
Have I not yet stopped my begging?

III.
HELP IN THE DARK SEASON

What blazes the trail
is not necessarily pretty.

—Mary Oliver

Heart Song II

I'm the white heron.
I'm the ginger root.

Wings wide in seamless
effort, floating high above.

Deep spice dug from soil,
built in darkness.

When I see my heart
it's a rose
made of charcoal.

The hole inside
is dark and the petals
wither around it.

But I spread my feathers
and my body dives down
into fire, where I remember—

The rose has a season
and look now, it's huge again,
pure red, singing within this small breast.

HOW LOVE LEARNS

When you first looked up at me
my breath paused for the hue
of cold blue stone. I touched
your shoulder. You came back
to find me before we were ready,
but that's how love learns.

There's a small hint of grief
when I say your name, when I walk
up to the grassy spot on the hill,
when I visit the place where we
wept into the dirt. It was the beginning—
I hadn't seen the way I leave my body,
and I hadn't gathered up enough
of anything to save us.

In my visions of our survival, I see
a house with a high wooden roof, tall
bookshelves, a thatched yellow chair,
worn blue jeans, brown socks,
our shared olive complexion,
and a joint respect
for the beauty of Big Sur.
I find you in the way this daisy is drawn,
in the way the candle burns
and drips its orange wax,
in the way the cloud
is a painted pink stroke
across the grey sky.

You are color and shape.
But what about being
a solid someone
who knows how to touch me
when I need it, who can stare
into my eyes without looking away?
I'm made of words,
my lifeblood is wrapped
in letters and I need your voice.
I don't have what it takes
to understand the nuance
of your silence.

NO NEW DICKS

I never want to see another new dick.
Methodical, I run through
my catalogue of names
and try to call this man
by the right one, but my magic
is limp and the list is far too lengthy.
My mind is a crowded hourglass.
To stop the spilling of sand
I have to release my hands,
let it all settle. Even if he fits
like an earth-key made
to unlock me, I must find
my own wand buried deep
within the heartwood
of my singular, perfect body.
But I keep coming back
to his and his and his.
This salt is not the same as ambrosia,
no matter how natural or obedient,
it's not sweet. I'm done being the witness,
the coffin and the collector. At long last
I'm in need of space. Skin is a popular
masterpiece, like clay living for my touch,
but my ledger is full.

Nearly Done Trying to Live

The pepper tree makes diamonds
of morning light, each branch
is wet with rainbow and the pink pearls
fall off in clumps. I climb
the hill across the street,
following the thin cut of trail
made by coyote paws. I curl up
in their den of matted grass.
Where are they in the daytime
while I'm giving up? I retreat into
the great valley of myself.
I can see my house from here,
the carpet where I rest and bite
my wrist, the altar where I let
another voice pass through.
The vines grow up over me
and the pack comes home at dusk.
We growl at each other softly, haunting
the night with our moving
tongues and teeth.
Because I'm empty, they let me stay.
I slip back down while they
eat the neighbor's chicken.
I consider that I may have parchment
in my bones and a mind made
of white boxes covered in dust.
Collections of junk replacing
the meat of my being.
Can I bring it back? My body
nourished and returned to flesh?
I may hold out my arm on the path
and see who considers me real
enough for a mouthful of blood.
For now, I get into bed
with the man and the cat.
I wait here for something new

that rises with the blank moon,
a mysterious reason
that prowls my spirit
and convinces me to stay.

I'm Not Your Boyfriend

I would have married you already
if I were a man. Fifteen years
of walking carefully around your lessons,
delivering bouquets of flowers, pulling
the golden strands of your hair from
my clothes. I nurtured each sign
of wisdom, bought you tarot cards,
cast spells and lit candles shaped
like hearts while envisioning
the best suitor, a cowboy walking
through the night to find you.
I finally see that it's not my job
to love you like this and I lay
my sword at your feet.
You can guard yourself in this battle
and I'll wait in the cave
where our conversations are preserved
in dark rock, where I'll keep the fire lit.

HEART ROCK

On the bank of the Trinity River
I find a heart shaped rock,
perfectly smooth
with a big scar in the center.
I used to fill my pockets with treasure:
pebbles, shells, bones and bark.
Now I just hold each one
and put it back where
it came from, a prayer
to remain in place.
But this worn stone,
with its distinct injury slightly
shining in the sun, comes home
with me. It sits in the center
of my altar and I coddle it
every morning. I cup it gently
and it exists as a unruined symbol
of ongoing work, the might
of mending that is left
in my hands alone.

A WAVE OF RESISTANCE

In one of my contrarian moods,
while walking up the steepest hill
in the neighborhood, I start to cut you down.
For every one of your great ideas, I have
the forgotten angle, my mother living
in each closed word. The butterflies
came today, painted ladies by the hundreds.
A sign, they inspire me to quit speaking.
I'm working on loving the part
of myself that I hate the most.

Common Place

Out my window I see two
tall, incongruous trees, one palm
and one Italian cypress. I lie
on the floor and masturbate
as the cat flicks his tail nearby.
The men on the street
are fixing the electricity, they drill
into wooden panels and speak Spanish.
The birds are singing, crows
and chickadees. I'm rubbing
a rhythm to conjure energy,
calling the voice of Goddess into my body,
asking this entrance to be illuminating.
I see the atoms spread as pointillism.
The trees' roots are inside of me
and the drill moves right through
to the core, past flesh and blood.
A man coughs for far too long, the dogs
start barking, and I'm finished,
no more wise than when I began,
but awake with some new-old fire.

THE WAY MY WINGS HAVE CHANGED

I sit under the full moon
in the silent desert and close my eyes
to see the door in my heart.
A small chamber without light,
I've accidentally locked a dragon inside.
His wings are mine—
wide span of scaled skin
across hollow bones, dark protection
casting a continent of shadow.
I release him into the night sky
and he comes back for a kiss,
nodding at the new gifts springing
from my shoulders, blade-like
and white, tall enough to reach the stars.
Now like an angelic warrior, I feel myself
grow, I release some of my defense.
But if I'm not the dragon, what's my work?
Back in my room, months later,
the wings turn limp and feathered.
Heaven must be relaxing into me.
I place my head on the ground
and cry relief. Look how gentle
these arms are when they aren't
in flight. After hibernation
they rise up again, extending
like never before, and I find myself
floating, ready to be this good bird.

PARTNERS

We unpack the people
who made us and can't find
anything amusing. Trauma stifles
humor, but we've been funny together,
dancing in the living room, laughing
at the yam singing in the oven.

I memorized your hands
the moment we met.
They hung above the typewriter
and reminded me
of horses, elegant and stern.
Cream-colored mares
that turn blue in the cold.
I wanted to hold them.
But years passed and we became
too close to trace each other's bodies.

That was back when we
needed to be perfect.
Now I get to love you
as we sob, shedding hair
and weight. Exchanging
survival sentences,
tethered to a reminder:
we are the same kind of mushroom,
alien to most, but glowing
under the surface, bearing
everything. Together
we're whittling our newness,
but partnership doesn't need
to look like two stable people
building something.
It can look simply
like us.

TOGETHER

Come over to my house.
The front door is ajar.
Enter and find me on my knees,
limp and weeping. Kneel with me.
Let us build our harmonies here.
Wallow with me and bite into grief.
After we have drenched our clothes,
after all is touched by the taste
of our uncontrollable salt—
we cradle one another.
We rise up, interlocked,
nearly ready to feel ready,
and then mourning turns
tactile, like ripe peaches
in our mouths. Words
drop heavy from our lips
and suddenly we find
the sweetness.
We hum.
We sing.
We lock eyes and taste
our singular breath,
inhale, exhale, sob harder
in praise that cracks at our
chests, joyous in our being.
For if we are alive—and we are—
we can conjure up
some spell of change
to split the seams of darkness,
to call in a new light
as we do, again
and again and again
and again,
together.

PERCIPLE

The wolf boy led me to you in fall
and by winter he'd moved on
to younger flesh. I started
coming back alone. Following
the cut of soil woven through
snow berries, I'd round the corner
and cry. A swollen temple of forty trunks,
you contained it all—a kitchen, a closet,
an altar, and most importantly
a bedroom where my body fit
in a slot with moss, a narrow casket.
I brought an offering each time,
filled your cup with crystals,
bobby pins and buttons.
I slept inside of you, wrapped
in a sleeping bag and tarp, reading
Whitman, eating soup from a thermos,
and rubbing myself. It wasn't until
spring that you told me your name.
I started licking bark, kissing roots,
collecting samaras, those winged seeds
that aided my angelic belief.
I drew symbols on your naked stag
with a ballpoint pen and wrapped
a colored sash there, as high
as I could climb. We were married
when your leaves were green,
my emblem of the earth, this place
my greatest love. I found a few notes
stuffed into a hole, signs of others
who adored your throne.
That's okay, I have others, too, but no
human could be you. If I marry
a person, the ritual will start here.
We'll kneel for permission and bow
into the taste of soil. Once I encircled you

with fallen sticks, wept and bled
at your feet. Now I see you changing.
Your limbs age with every visit, on each
pilgrimage I find the weight of time
revealing itself, sagging boughs, the entire
kitchen broken into rot. You don't need
a singular body to be my spouse. We protect
each other from afar, even as we're dying,
my husband, my wife, my god.
My one and only maple.

THE ABLE MAN

I so often put the cat
before the man.
When I walk in the door
my voice rises like a whistle
for this little black and white
animal and then I slump
into the man's arms, spent
from a day out in the world.
Does he get the worst of me?
The cat won't let me hold him,
he slices my finger in jest, bites
my forearm until it bleeds,
and demands a drink
from the faucet at three a.m.
Why do I serve him so?
He can't speak.
He's otherworldly.
He's closer to the ground
and akin to things
beyond human grasp.
In bed, there's one fluid motion:
the man stirs in his sleep,
I sit up and put my hand
on the cat's back so he doesn't get kicked,
and then we're all dreaming again.
Who am I but a protector?
The cat is easy.
He arrived on my doorstep
to teach me how to love unconditionally.
The lesson transfers slowly
into other relationships.
The man's wisdom is one
of effort, this battle to push down
the panels that surround my heart

so he can have the honor
of holding it. He shows me
he's able. He learns to love the cat
without question.

THE WORK THAT CANNOT BE DONE ALONE

I'm so much happier
when I'm by myself. I can go
at least seven days without seeing
another human. I'm the hermit
in the desert, but I eventually ache
to show the sunrise to someone.
The work of love proves
that I'm more than a gritty animal.
I see the hole in my heart
fill with ash when you arrive,
a sign that I need to be held.
My brain cannot grow
without your eyes staring into mine.
I cannot be good without knowing
how to surrender, how to let you
be both a child and a man in my arms.
Relationships are a cosmic handout.
A challenge sits between me and my lover—
an infinity mirror that I can withstand
only because this person knows
when to cover my face.
Togetherness reveals a realm
as deep and hot as a volcano.
We'll burn up in there
if we do it right.

It Can Be Better Than You Ever Hoped

Love can start in childhood
and take its time, twenty years
to grow into a thing so reliable
it need not cover itself with a sheet.
It can arrive in the form of a man
who has smooth skin, who will make you juice
every morning, who will tell you
about what's happening in the outside world
when you cannot leave the cave.
He can be a person who withstands
your waves of resistance, who has words
for the moments that matter, who can pull
your stinger from his arm again and again
and simply say *I don't appreciate that.*
He doesn't let you carve him into
something small and he speaks to you
during sex saying *you're safe, you're safe,*
an answer brought forth by prayer.

How We Stay

i.

A hand made out of graphite
on my throat, a braid
of lead in my chest,
and deep scratches
on my wrists
that look like lace.

When I argue
with the outcome of the day,
when I'm wholly
bludgeoned by being,
I imagine smacking my skull
hard against the window.

When swimming, I sink under
and hum low desire:
make me a blade of eel grass
hitched to the ocean floor
or just let me forever sleep
in the curl of a wave.

ii.

When you called me from Texas,
hardly breathing, it was morning
and I'm always better in the morning.
I was wearing my black robe
and ascended the staircase
willing to show you
a reason
to stay alive.

Why should we not drink poison?
They sip our light like water, they've buried us
more than once already, so why
would we continue clawing?

The mystery keeps us here.
We are an amalgamation
of atoms, each of us
is the entire universe
doing its thing.

iii.

Your survival is my own.
I never wanted a child
before I saved you.
Now, having felt life
pass through my body,
how could I say no to something
so unfathomable and determined?
Whatever wants to move
in and out of me, whatever shape
it needs to take in order to weave
its tangled story, I stand here saying
who am I to get in its way,
who am I to stop it?

TO SEE IT BETTER

Why in a poem are we always trying
to relate the subject matter to something else?
I stare at the insane hill of grass
that is not a normal sight in Los Angeles,
blades two fingers thick, and it's like some collection of sultry hands,
curves of thin kelly and lime that feel like horse mane,
but it needs no relation. It's been asleep in the driest dirt
for who knows how long and so suddenly,
with strange, relentless rain, it rises up,
tips as red as madder root,
and I love it for itself.

No Longer Desperation

You can keep on wanting love,
but you can no longer hunt it.
Go ahead and name the exact form
of devotion that makes sense to you.
Write down what means the most,
what traits are not negotiable,
what passion and what purpose
must be attached to spirit.
Would he trade his life for the health of the planet?
Does she indulge in long periods of solitude and silence?
Could he kill the chicken he loves to eat?
Will she point out the white horse in the pasture?
Accept that love will appear in a way
that you can never fully imagine.
Now call it in with your own voice.
Invite it to reside with you.
Don't grasp or whine.
Don't beg or yowl.
The weight of your pleading
causes such a fine feeling to retreat.
Love wants to see
if you can love yourself alone
before it calls your heart its home.
Can it trust you to never clasp
too tightly? Can it believe
that you won't quit when shadow falls?
Will it arrive and see a thirst
or a well that's already brimming?
Get clear, list the details of your need,
bring in nothing less than this perfection.
Love won't like it if you've been wasting time
on those who don't honor it.
It'll call you a fool and a traitor.
It'll see your hunger and curl closer into itself.
Let love know you're already full,

let it see how you're saturated
in your own delight. Show it
the looseness around your craving
that leaves space for possibility.

HOW TO FALL IN LOVE WITH YOURSELF

Sit in front of two candles,
one for each eye.
Light them and watch how the fire
takes its time with the wicks, nearly dying,
touching wax and climbing back into air
with a wave of hot yes.
Now, breathe each flame into the crown
of your head. There is a hole there
where elements can enter.
Your skull is a cup, hungry for light.
Close your eyes and let
this glowing gift travel throughout
your entire body, take it down
slowly, like a dose of brilliant honey.
See how you overflow?
See how you do magic?
The warmth is red. It's white, orange,
blue and green. It touches every
part of you and when
the tailbone starts snaking,
when you become a tree,
you will love yourself completely
for burning with such ease.

LORD'S KIN

The voice of God calls me *Child*.
As in *hush Child* or *you're alright Child*.
The words come out of my own mouth.
I am my own God speaking, cooing soothing comfort.
To be the baby of life and realize the universe is parenting me.
I am *Child* when I weep. I am *Child* when I lack
clarity and ask my tedious questions in the dark.
Shhhhh, there there, you are breathing, you are new again.

FUTURE

I can't see my future clearly.
It's a wash of color and light.
Maybe a glimpse of a house
with wood floors, the death
of a parent, a dog, a cat, a love,
but nothing certain. I like its fog.
Inevitably something will happen, pieces
will fall into place if I keep breathing
and I'll eat, I'll work, I'll learn
and know and forget. There'll be
another bowl full of berries, a hot cup
of tea, additional travel and sorrow.
There'll be a clean pair of pants,
the sun's good glow, a cut and blood,
a hole to dig, a bath to take, a mistake to mend.
What lies ahead is a promise
standing in shadow, one second
pasted to the next. I don't need to call it
by name. A riddle ensues, a song of guessing,
a vow of risk. The road becomes itself
single stone after single stone
made of limitless possibility,
endless awe.

ACKNOWLEDGMENTS

Thank you, Shelby Duncan, rock of my heart, my forever Queen, for walking through the darkness with me so willingly. May we always learn in unison on this everlasting journey. You deserve the greatest love imaginable.

Eric Fernandez, thank you for witnessing me, for holding space, for your valuable edits, your crucial vulnerability, your immense patience and your limitless love. You are truly a gift. You've seen just the beginning of my breaking open, and I know it's horrific at times, I know it's hard. You are a sacred part of the process and I appreciate you wholly.

Nicole Disson and Mariana Blanco, thank you for giving me a sense of home, for calling me family, for letting me be your teenage son, and for nurturing me when I need it. Knowing that I have your reliable love is a true comfort.

Thank you, Skylar Hughes, for all the years of sifting through, for the hardest heart-work, for lasting friendship. You are my family and my favorite artist. I'll always support and love you. I'll always be here to grow with you.

Thank you again Matt Phipps, for being my dear friend and lifelong editing partner, for accepting the work of this manuscript with openness and love. I couldn't do it without your tender help.

Chelsea Bayouth, I cannot conjure up enough words of gratitude for your last-minute editing expertise. I needed a woman's eye on this work and you gave me yours with such heartfelt dedication.

Derrick C. Brown, I'm so grateful you asked me to write a book of poems about love for Write Bloody. Out of that request came the brutal work of unraveling trauma, and a collection of poetry that resulted in a healing catharsis. Thank you so much for the opportunity to delve into these parts of myself that so needed to live on the page.

Jeff Warrin, we gave definition to the dark season. Our time together pushed me over the edge, into a world of healing I hadn't been able to access. After all of the pain, I'm held in a wave of gratitude to know you, to have grown together, to have withstood and transformed from the heart on out.

Thank you to all of my incredible friends who continue to keep me in the light as I move through this often unbearable process— Particularly my LC Elena Stonaker, George Augusto, Jesse Klein Seret, Tessa Thompson, Carly Jo Morgan, Jena Malone, Brooke Boston, Liz Kimbrough, Erielle Laniewski, Sacha Marini, Rachel Zingone, Yasmine Khatib, Jenny O., Geneviève Medow-Jenkins, Grantopolis Gardner, Emily J. Synder, Wade Ryff, Zachary Houston, Angela de la Agua, Jules Blaine Davis, Lauren Morlock, Kyle W. Sweetgum Alabama, Sarah Sky, Kate Moss, Natasha Rocas, Krishna Mali and Tio.

Thank you to Priest G. for the most incredible and cosmic bond. By knowing you, I'm reminded of the reasons that help me stay the course every step of the way.

I'm grateful for all of the healthy couples in my life who show me what true, resilient love looks like—Especially Rick & Beth, Naomi & John, Matt & Lucy, Michael & Melanie, Chris & Susan, Hallie & Jack, Nicole & Mariana, Karen & Harold, Chris & Dale, Steve & Judy, Chris & Floor, and Jesse & Isaiah.

There are a few grown women in my life who have shown me moments of unconditional, nurturing, and parental love. Without you, I wouldn't know what it feels like to be a beloved child—Naomi Dallob, Karen Walden, Chris Hughes, Susan Gates, Marion Lasley, Sharon Comkowycz, Anya Laniewski, Ginny Grimsley, my late grandmother Jean Martin and of course my Doda.

I thank Wayne Stevens and Lisa Barr for being part of my familial journey. I learned huge lessons from both of you and am deeply grateful.

I'm thankful for all of the healers who have helped me along the way, especially Helena Vissing, Leona Marrs, Juniper Garza and Dana Griffin. Therapy, in whatever form, is a crucial art and a practice that I deeply recommend.

A few years ago, Marlee Grace taught a workshop called *Help in the Dark Season* and thus, the title of this book is her creation. Marlee, you are my soulmate, especially in the practice of creative healing, and I love you.

The last two lines of the poem "A Wave of Resistance" are inspired by the Twain song "Hank & Georgia." Twain's music has been a steadfast component of my healing work.

The title "It Can Be Better Than You Ever Hoped" is a line by the writer Bethany Toews.

To everyone I've loved, to all of you I've hurt, to anyone who hurt me, I thank you for the love and the lessons. Each moment, each word exchanged, all of it adds up to show me the magic of being alive, the power of healing, the patterns of the subconscious, and I'm grateful. I'm also sorry. I'm working with quite a tangle here. One thing that I know for certain is that if I ever loved you, I still love you.

To my parents, I'm very glad to be alive on planet earth. Even if life is a job that requires heart-wrenching work, even if it takes me many lifetimes to unlearn your ways, I'm in awe of it all and I'm thankful for this chance to be here, exactly as I am.

ABOUT THE AUTHOR

JACQUELINE SUSKIN is a poet and educator based in Los Angeles. She is the author of *The Collected*, *Go Ahead & Like It*, *The Edge of the Continent Volume One: The Forest*, and *The Edge of the Continent Volume Two: The City*. Known for her project Poem Store, Suskin composes improvisational poetry for patrons who choose a topic in exchange for a unique verse. Poem Store has been her main occupation since 2009 and has taken her around the world writing nearly forty thousand spontaneous poems. She was honored by Michelle Obama at the White House as a Turnaround Artist, and her work has been featured in *New York Times*, *T Magazine*, *Los Angeles Times*, *The Atlantic*, and various other publications.

www.jacquelinesuskin.com

If You Like Jacqueline Suskin, Jacqueline Likes...

Hello. It Doesn't Matter.
Derrick C. Brown

Counting Descent
Clint Smith

Some of the Children Were Listening
Lauren Sanderson

In Search of Midnight
Mike McGee

Open Your Mouth Like a Bell
Mindy Nettifee

Write Bloody Publishing publishes and promotes great books of poetry every year. We believe that poetry can change the world for the better. We are an independent press dedicated to quality literature and book design, with an office in Los Angeles, California.

We are grassroots, DIY, bootstrap believers. Pull up a good book and join the family. Support independent authors, artists, and presses.

Want to know more about Write Bloody books, authors, and events? Join our mailing list at

www.writebloody.com

WRITE BLOODY BOOKS

After the Witch Hunt — Megan Falley

Aim for the Head: An Anthology of Zombie Poetry — Rob Sturma, Editor

Amulet — Jason Bayani

Any Psalm You Want — Khary Jackson

Atrophy — Jackson Burgess

Birthday Girl with Possum — Brendan Constantine

The Bones Below — Sierra DeMulder

Born in the Year of the Butterfly Knife — Derrick C. Brown

Bouquet of Red Flags — Taylor Mali

Bring Down the Chandeliers — Tara Hardy

Ceremony for the Choking Ghost — Karen Finneyfrock

A Constellation of Half-Lives — Seema Reza

Counting Descent — Clint Smith

Courage: Daring Poems for Gutsy Girls — Karen Finneyfrock,
Mindy Nettifee, & Rachel McKibbens, Editors

Dear Future Boyfriend — Cristin O'Keefe Aptowicz

Do Not Bring Him Water — Caitlin Scarano

Don't Smell the Floss — Matty Byloos

Drive Here and Devastate Me — Megan Falley

Drunks and Other Poems of Recovery — Jack McCarthy

The Elephant Engine High Dive Revival — Derrick C. Brown, Editor

Everyone I Love Is a Stranger to Someone — Annelyse Gelman

Everything Is Everything — Cristin O'Keefe Aptowicz

Favorite Daughter — Nancy Huang

The Feather Room — Anis Mojgani

Floating, Brilliant, Gone — Franny Choi

Glitter in the Blood: A Poet's Manifesto for Better, Braver Writing — Mindy Nettifee

Gold That Frames the Mirror — Brandon Melendez

The Heart of a Comet — Pages D. Matam

CPSIA information can be obtained
at www.ICGtesting.com
Printed in the USA
FSHW011502300121